**The Let's Talk Library**™

# Let's Talk About Feeling Embarrassed

Melanie Ann Apel

The Rosen Publishing Group's
**PowerKids Press**™
New York

For Katie Kocelko, a true inspiration. Love, Melanie.

Published in 2001 by The Rosen Publishing Group, Inc.
29 East 21st Street, New York, NY 10010

First Edition

Book design: Maria Melendez

Photo credits: Cover and title page, pp. 7, 11, 12, 16, 20 © Shalhevet Moshe; pp. 4, 8, 19 © Skjold Photographs; pp. 15 © Tony Stone Images;

Apel, Melanie Ann.
    Let's talk about being embarrassed/ by Melanie Ann Apel.
        p. cm.—(The let's talk about library)
    Includes index.
    Summary: Discusses the physical and psychological effects of feeling embarrassed and how to deal with the emotion.
    ISBN 0-8239-5618-0  (lib. bdg. : alk. paper)
    1. Embarrassment in children—Juvenile literature. [1. Embarrassment.] I. Title. II. Series.
BF723.E44 A64 2000
152.4—dc21                                    99-055038

Manufactured in the United States of America

# Table of Contents

# Lisa

Lisa has been practicing shooting basketballs with her older brother Alex. Alex tells Lisa's friends that now she gets a lot more basketballs through the hoop. Lisa's friends want her to show them how she has improved. Lisa is nervous about shooting baskets in front of her friends. She is afraid that if she misses the basket her friends will make fun of her. Lisa would feel **embarrassed** if her friends laughed at her.

◄ *A lot of people get nervous when they are the center of attention.*

# What Is Embarrassment?

**Embarrassment** is a feeling of **confusion** or **discomfort**. Have you ever done something that didn't go the way you planned? Maybe you licked your ice-cream cone too hard and the ice cream fell off the cone and onto the floor. Did that make you feel sad or bad about yourself? Did you worry that someone might laugh at you or not like you? If you felt this way, you were feeling embarrassed.

*Things don't always go the way you planned. Try not to feel bad about yourself for making a mistake.* ▶

# Who Feels Embarrassed?

Everyone feels embarrassed sometimes. You might feel embarrassed if you say something wrong, like calling your friend by the wrong name. You might feel embarrassed if you trip and fall down. Getting a haircut that you think looks bad can also make you feel embarrassed. People may feel embarrassed for a lot of reasons. They may worry about what other people will think of them.

◄ *When you feel embarrassed, remember you are not alone. Everyone has times when they feel embarrassed.*

# Keith's Brother

Keith's mom says it is time to leave the playground. Jared, Keith's brother, wants to stay. He throws himself on the ground and starts to cry loudly. He makes a big fuss. Keith's best friend Mark stops playing and stares at Jared. Keith wishes Jared would stop fussing. He is embarrassed by the way his brother is acting.

*When someone you are with makes a fuss, you might feel embarrassed.* ▶

# Being Embarrassed by Someone Else

Sometimes what other people do embarrasses you. Keith was embarrassed when his brother Jared made a fuss. Keith wasn't doing anything to embarrass himself. He felt embarrassed because everyone was looking at Jared. He worried that his friend might think he would act as badly as his brother. Keith should understand that he is not responsible for the way Jared acts.

◀ *You can't control how someone else acts. Don't let what they do make you feel bad about yourself.*

# Feeling Different

People might feel embarrassed because they don't look like everyone else. Molly is embarrassed because she is the only girl in her ballet class who doesn't have a pink leotard. Her leotard is purple. Molly and her friend Hannah are getting ready for class at Molly's house. Hannah asks Molly why her leotard is purple. Molly says that the store was out of pink ones. Molly is afraid that Hannah will laugh at her. Instead, Hannah says, "I wish my leotard was purple. I love that color!" Molly sees that looking different doesn't have to be a bad thing.

*You don't have to look or act like anyone else to be accepted. People will like you for being you.* ▶

# What Happens When You Feel Embarrassed?

Kelly is embarrassed. When she feels embarrassed her face turns red. She looks down, away from everyone else's eyes. She feels stupid and wants to cry. She even thinks about running away. This is how a person can feel when he or she is embarrassed.

Feeling embarrassed, like feeling angry or sad, is painful. The bad feelings will go away, though. Soon Kelly will feel better. Bad feelings hurt, but it is important to remember that they won't last forever.

◀ *Being embarrassed hurts, but the bad feelings will go away.*

# Your Self-Esteem

People who have a strong sense of **self-esteem** don't feel embarrassed very often. They know that everyone makes mistakes. They know that it is okay to do things differently or to look different from other people. Try not to worry about how other people will **react** if you do something wrong or in a different way. If you feel good about yourself, what other people think will not matter so much. You also won't feel as embarrassed when things don't go the way you expect.

*Playing sports is one way to feel good about yourself.* ▶

# Being Prepared

Ethan is worried about playing the wrong notes at his piano **recital**. He thinks that if he makes a mistake everyone will laugh at him and he will be too embarrassed to finish playing. Ethan practices the piano whenever he has free time. By the day of the recital, he is making very few mistakes.

Being prepared for what you are going to do will help you avoid an embarrassing situation. Ethan practiced hard. He did not make many mistakes when he played the piano at the recital. He did not feel embarrassed.

◀ *If you prepare for things, there is less chance you will make mistakes and feel embarrassed.*

# Being Yourself

Remember that it is natural to feel embarrassed sometimes. You can learn to laugh at yourself and your mistakes. No one is perfect and everyone makes mistakes. You do not have to feel embarrassed about mistakes. Try not to worry so much about what other people think. Do your best, but remember that things don't always work out the way you expect. As long as you try to do well, you have nothing to be embarrassed about.

# Glossary

**confusion** (kun-FYOO-jhun)  Feeling unsure about something.

**discomfort** (dis-KUM-furt)  Feeling awkward or uncomfortable.

**embarrassed** (im-BAYR-ist)  Feeling uncomfortable or ashamed.

**embarrassment** (im-BAYR-uhs-ment)  A feeling of shame or uneasiness.

**react** (re-AKT)  How someone responds to something.

**recital** (ree-SY-tul)  A concert given by a musician.

**self-esteem** (SELF-uh-STEEM)  How you feel about yourself.

# Index